The Music of Love

Judith Pinhey

Robert Llewep.

The Music of Love

Images of the Risen Jesus

Judith Pinhey

Edited by Robert Llewelyn

Collins
FOUNT PAPERBACKS

First published in Great Britain by Fount Paperbacks, London in 1990

Copyright © Judith Pinhey 1990

Typeset by Avocet Robinson, Buckingham
Printed and bound in Great Britain by
William Collins Sons & Co. Ltd, Glasgow

Contents

Editor's Foreword

If you want to be drenched in the love of God sit quietly for a space before the imagery of this book. Let its pages flood over you as healing waters; let them enwrap you as a friendly cloak. On every page the love of God shines through: warm, energizing, compassionate, strong and true. Here is a treasure store of imagery and wealth which, whilst it retains an individuality of its own, is comparable in substance and beauty with memorable passages from the classics of the spiritual life.

When in the spring of this year I received from Judith Pinhey pages from the beautifully written manuscript which lies behind this book it was at once clear that here were writings of exceptional quality. Later I was able to meet the writer herself; to receive the full manuscript and to learn how it came to be written. I was shortly to visit Medugorje in Yugoslavia, and knowing that Teresa de Bertodano, editor of Collins Fount, would be on our party, I decided to take the manuscript to show her. She was quick to confirm my judgement that the writings, shared hitherto with only a circle of friends, should be made available to as wide a readership as possible. It was in this way that, with the writer's consent (she had not originally thought of publication), this book found its beginnings.

It is not an ordinary book, as the reader who cares to move forward to any of its pages will rapidly discover. Nor was it written in an ordinary way, as I now write this introduction, sitting before the work and searching for words to convey my meaning. Some of us have considerable difficulty in setting down our thoughts for others to read, and Judith Pinhey would count herself among them. Yet here, page after page, are effortless writings of great freshness and clarity, simple in expression yet profound in their meaning, enkindling the spirit and drawing the heart to its resting place in God in an ever deepening bond of intimacy and love.

The writings which form the substance of this book belong to a class known to theology as interior locution. Such locutions – some may prefer to call them revelations – take two forms known as imaginative and intellectual: these writings belong to the former class. In an imaginative locution the receiver experiences words being formed in the imagination or understanding clearly and distinctly, so that he or she may speak them or write them down. Julian of Norwich experienced this type of locution when receiving the showings which are the foundation of her *Revelations of Divine Love* "All this was shown", she writes, "in three parts, by bodily vision, *by words formed in my understanding*, and by spiritual vision". And again, "our Lord very humbly revealed words to me, without voice and without opening of lips, just as he had done before, and said . . ."*
Here Julian clearly distinguishes between an exterior and an interior locution, both of which were known to her. In an exterior locution a voice is heard as though the speaker is present and the receiver imagines that anyone standing by would be able to hear the voice as well. Judith Pinhey has in her lifetime received only one exterior locution, as her poignantly moving introduction reveals. In the interior locution to which Julian has here referred there was no voice heard, as it were, with her ears, but simply the formation of words within, and Julian was clear that it was the risen Jesus who was speaking to her. This precisely describes Judith Pinhey's case, and with Julian she is assured – and

*My italics in each case. The passages may be found in chapters 9 and 68 of *Julian of Norwich: Showings*, edited by Edmund Colledge OSA and James Walsh SJ, SPCK, London, 1978.

I share her assurance — that the source of the revelation is Jesus himself. Why she should have been chosen remains a mystery, but the answer of her heart is that God often accomplishes his purpose through the least of his people that the greatness of his power may be known.

Locutions are commonplace in the Bible though the word itself does not appear. The many passages in the Old Testament beginning with such words as, "The voice of the Lord came to me saying" must often betoken a locutionary experience, though of what class it may not be possible to determine. The messages will depend on the circumstances of the time and will in some degree be coloured by the character and background of the one who receives them. Hosea differs from Amos, but in each case it is God who speaks.

In the New Testament the book of "Revelation" is saturated with locutionary and visionary experiences. Locution accompanied with corporeal vision is also a prominent feature of the resurrection stories. But there are, too, a number of other examples scattered through the gospels and the narrative of the early Church.

Locutions, though in no way necessary to the spiritual life, have an honourable place in the traditions of the Church: many examples, too, might be quoted from the present time. Not every locution, however, is of divine origin. A psychological disorder may account for some, evil or wandering spirits for others. St John tells us (1 John 4:1-4) that we are to test the spirits whether they are of God. The overruling mark of the present book is the exaltation of Jesus as Lord. The scriptural assurance of God's never failing love revealed in the teaching, death and resurrection of Jesus rings out through its pages.

I believe that the power of these passages to bind up and to heal is inseparably linked, in the mystery of God's providence, with the suffering which Judith and her family have been called upon to bear. In an unaffectedly beautiful introduction Judith has, at my request, told what has been laid upon her. Even so it is not quite the whole story, nor may that be made known to all at the present time. Once again Julian's words come to our help. "The remedy is that our Lord is with us and leading us into the fullness of joy . . . And he gave understanding of this . . . especially in the revelation of his Passion"** Here in this book is the message that the joy of the resurrection life is to be found through the glad acceptance of the cross – God help us all – and not in the attempted smoothing of the path in self-regarding and self-chosen ways. I hope that these words may be heard throughout the world by all to whom they may bring strength and assurance, enrichment and joy.

ROBERT LLEWELYN

** Ibid. Chapter 77.

Introduction

I began to receive these words in November 1985 when I was forty-nine, and I believe that they are given by the risen Lord Jesus. He is the Word of God, and he says "I love you" in a variety of ways. He humbly comes into our hearts and minds in the way that is most natural for each of us. I can only try to explain how he speaks to me, but you will know how he speaks to you.

All my life I had wanted to be able to pray but I could not summon up the motivation or relax enough to spend one minute in quiet. Whenever I read a book on prayer I would think "That's marvellous!" but I could not put it into practice. I wanted to know God, not merely to know about him, and little by little he led me on.

I taught from 1970 to 1987 at St Mary's Convent Junior School in Cambridge, and learnt at least as much as I taught. One day a colleague was leading a meditation and said, "Now in silence let us tell God that we love him". I could not do that and I could not forget it. I believe that God gave me that dissatisfaction, that desire and eventually that desperation. In August 1985, as I was scraping window frames at home for painting, I said aloud, "O God, you'll have to do something because I can't".

Alongside a looking towards God more expectantly was a looking inward more honestly. God led me in that direction as well, and I prayed, "I'm fed up with being so self-conscious. I want to be conscious only of you".

At the beginning of the autumn half-term holiday that year I bought a book which I had seen reviewed. I was curious to know what it was about. It was *Power Evangelism* by John Wimber, and he made Jesus seem so attractive and real that I longed to know him in that way. By the afternoon of Saturday 26th October I had reached the end of chapter 9 where I read: "All that is required is your co-operation in opening your heart to God and asking the Spirit to fill you and take control of your life." At last I understood that I could ask for the help I needed and receive it, so I asked. My intention was to give myself into God's hands as far as was in me. Then I made a cup of tea. I had no idea what I had asked for.

That evening, while I was in the bath, suddenly and totally unexpectedly I heard with my ears the words: "Peace, be still." I knew that it was Jesus who had spoken to me and that he had given me a very deep inner healing from stress and tension. My husband, Jonathan, said later, "You've changed from a pessimist into an optimist", and my doctor told me that at least two-fifths of her patients need this kind of healing and she cannot help them. I also found that I could kneel for the first time for twenty years because my back and knee were free from pain and this healing has been maintained.

This is the only occasion when I have heard words with my ears, and I believe that the Holy Spirit activated my hearing.

The next day, in our church, at the eucharist, as I received the bread, Jesus showed me his love. The fire of his love shone right into the depths of my being and set my heart on fire with love for him. It was as if my penfriend had become my lover. Now the knowledge of his love and the joy of his presence are always with me.

It is the gracious work of the Holy Spirit to glorify Jesus and to reveal him to us, and I understand this experience as coming out of the riches of God's grace available to me in my baptism. It was a spiritual awakening and a new beginning.

As I was full of love and praise for my Lord that Sunday

afternoon, I noticed a contraction of the muscles of the throat and the back of the tongue, firm but comfortable. I had no way of knowing what this meant, but about a month later I realized that words were coming very clearly into my mind, not thoughts formed by me but words formed within me. I believed then, and I believe now, that these words are given by Jesus who is alive and active through his Spirit. As the passages became longer I learnt to write them down, phrase by phrase, sentence by sentence, like dictation. It is still the same: when the contraction begins I listen, or when I listen the contraction begins. The words continue until the end of the passage and then the contraction releases.

The words come out of silence, out of a gift of contemplation. I listen attentively in my heart, with my mind alert. When the words begin, sometimes gently, sometimes bursting into my consciousness, I do not know what the passage will be about, how it will develop or how long it will be, but the words make sense; as they proceed they hang together and by the end they make a whole. I may receive words anywhere. If I am cooking I do not leave the saucepans to burn and if I am on my bicycle I do not endanger the traffic, but at the next opportunity I write them down. If I am interrupted in the middle of a passage it will continue later. Sometimes the words flow, sometimes there are silences. A passage of average length may take fifteen minutes or perhaps about half an hour.

When I am composing a piece of writing it is completely different. A letter or an article is quite a labour for me as I have never been able to write anything straight out. My husband always teases me about the number of rough drafts I need to make, hacking and pruning paragraphs, grafting in sentences and transplanting words. The passages I receive come ready-made and remain as I receive them. I would not be capable of writing them myself.

At first it was acutely embarrassing to disclose these words. It felt almost like going around naked. At the same time there is a strong urge in me to give them to others. I have always been glad that they are in the first person because it is obvious that Jesus is speaking as much to me as to anyone through me.

People have sometimes asked, "Why you?" – a fair question since I have no theological qualification and no office or status in the church. My husband and I are ordinary members of St James' Church, Cambridge, where we have worshipped for almost twenty years. I can only answer "Why not?" Anything that we receive from God is undeserved, a gift of his grace, to be received with thanksgiving and used. All the different kinds of service we offer are needed. This is my service. I need your service. We all need each other.

I am also asked whether it is frightening to receive these words and I can answer wholeheartedly, "Not at all". It feels like something I was made for. I never know Jesus as angry with me or with anyone else. What he always shows me is his overflowing, unconditional love and tender mercy for me and for all the world.

This love is so real that it is no kind of insurance against suffering; rather it is a call to suffer and involves us in suffering. This is another strand in my story.

My husband and I have been married for thirty years. We have two married daughters and a son who now lives with us so that he can be cared for.

Nicholas is twenty-seven and is a severe longterm sufferer from Myalgic Encephalomyelitis (M.E.) sometimes known as Post Viral Fatigue Syndrome. Until he became ill in 1983, when he was twenty-one, he was fit, energetic, able, sociable and full of fun. Now he is so limited by the disease that he has to lie on his back in great pain, unable to open his eyes even in a darkened room. He is isolated and very lonely. He can have an occasional visitor for a few minutes.

"Myalgic Encephalomyelitis" means "painful muscles and inflammation of the brain and spinal cord". The disease is caused by one of several possible viruses. Medical opinion is divided and there are conflicting views and theories about the treatment of symptoms. This is bewildering for patients and carers. Some research is being done but at present there is no cure. Most people recover within a few years, but for reasons still not understood, some do not.

Nicholas has intense pain in his head and eyes and in his infected sinuses. All his muscles below the waist are painful. He has spasms of the muscles above the waist and spasms of the gut. His memory, concentration and speech are affected, and so are some of the automatic functions of the brain: sleep pattern, temperature control, breathing and heart rate. Other unpleasant nervous disturbances include tingling and twitching and tinnitus. He is deeply exhausted all the time, and suffers from nausea and digestive problems. He is allergic to pain killers, and there are many other drugs, and some foods, that he cannot tolerate. He has recurring bouts of illness resulting each time in a worsening of his condition. Most of the symptoms fluctuate in a random way, so that repeatedly his hopes are raised only to be dashed.

Nicholas emphatically wants to be well and live a normal life, but equally, when he does not know how to bear one more hour of pain, he wants to die. Sometimes he talks of killing himself but he does not think he has a sure way of doing it. You do not die of M.E. but it can be a living death. When Nicholas feels angry, sad, frustrated, terrified or despairing he cannot gain relief by expressing these human emotions because to do so makes him worse. He feels he is in a straitjacket and he is often depressed. Most of the time, although he no longer knows God's presence for himself, he endures a dreadful disease with great courage.

When we first realized that Nicholas was not recovering I cried out to God continually, ''My son is ill. Aren't you going to do something?'' I thought I could never be happy until Nicholas was well. I had been healed. Why not

Nicholas? He needed it more. Why not Nicholas instead of me? Surely he had suffered enough. It was as if I was banging my head against a stone wall.

I had to face the fact that hundreds of people were faithfully praying for Nicholas and that God could most certainly hear us. He is not deaf, nor is he waiting for us to hit on the right prayer formula. I could not move God so I had to move. Somehow I had to reconcile the compassionate love of Jesus that I knew every day with the reality of Nicholas' illness.

Increasingly I find that to approach even a little way towards the edge of the mystery of the Christian faith, it is necessary to hold together in tension two opposites and that the resolution of every paradox is in the cross and nowhere else.

"Jesus! Where are you?" I shouted into the darkness. "On the cross" was the reply in my heart. When I look at the cross I see there that when Jesus suffered and died it was not a mistake which God later turned to good, nor did God merely allow it to happen, but it was his positive will, his plan from before creation. It is not possible to know the love of God without the cross because the cross has always been in his heart. I asked Jesus to teach me ever more deeply the meaning of his cross and I began to understand that all suffering – past, present and future – is contained in the cross and is like it. God wills and suffers the cross. I cannot take the God who suffers and leave the God who wills.

Sometimes in my imagination I see Jesus, afflicted with this disease to the same degree as Nicholas, lying beside him on the bed, like him in every respect, except that he has his arms round him.

Sometimes I say to God. "Nicholas is our son but he is also your son. Do with him what you will." Can I be surprised or affronted when I know what God did to his own Son? The way of the cross is always the way we do not want to go.

I do not know how to compare one kind of suffering with another, but I never forget that I am not the one who has to bear all this pain in myself. I bear it as an onlooker.

Suffering is always revelational. Through suffering Jesus is teaching me things I could learn in no other way, although I would not choose to learn them at Nicholas' expense.

I began to learn that since Nicholas' illness was something I could not change, I had to accept it – to accept, not grudgingly but willingly, the worst that could happen: a very severe illness with intense pain, lasting a very long time, perhaps indefinitely, perhaps throughout a long life. All I can say is, "Lord, I will love you whatever", and ask for his grace to live out the meaning of that commitment. I fail, but he knows my weakness and his love is unfailing love.

I used to be afraid, when I went into Nicholas' room, of what I would find and how I would cope with the latest setback, until one day Jesus said to me, "Fear is the contemplation of a place where I am not". I have found that there is no such place. He is in the reality of the anguish when I face it head on, not turning aside from it. By entering into the horror with open eyes, by acknowledging all the agony and submitting to it, by absorbing it into myself, I have discovered that the darkness is a place of peace, inner freedom and an inexplicable joy – the joy of the resurrection which is in the cross and not apart from it.

Suffering is also sacrificial. When I offer this suffering to be joined with the suffering of Jesus on the cross I believe that he can change it from something destructive into something creative. Who can say when suffering is too much, when the price to be paid is altogether too high?

A situation like this calls out so much love that otherwise could not have existed. Jonathan and I are together in caring for Nicholas and taking part in his suffering. We support each other and our love has grown. We are strengthened by the love and prayers, kindness and practical help of our family, our brothers and sisters at St James' and many friends. Without this we should not be able to manage.

I have learnt to accept Nicholas' illness for today and to ask for his healing for tomorrow. Since God's ultimate will is to heal I will never give up asking and hoping, but the timing is his.

It is possible that Nicholas may begin to improve. Some treatment may be found that will help him. The disease is beginning to be a little better understood and there may one day be a cure. These are sources of hope.

Beyond this my hope is in God himself. Evil is the risk he is prepared to take. It is the reality he is ultimately responsible for (as anyone who has cursed him in a state of dereliction knows full well) and he has proved his responsibility for it on the cross. For me, a God who wills to suffer to the ultimate is the ultimate answer to suffering. I am prepared to trust this God although I do not understand the mystery of suffering. If Jesus had not died on the cross, nothing would make sense and everything would be lost, but he did, and so everything, even here and now, is all right.

JUDITH PINHEY

August 1989

Editorial Note

The passages which follow are arranged in a chronological order and are selected from several hundred given to Judith Pinhey between 25 June 1986 and 10 July 1989. The date of each is not shown but the reader may like to know that *For the people of the USSR* was given on 24 July 1986, and *From Holy Russia my holiness will shine forth* on 23 January 1987.

R.L.

The music of heaven

Make music to me in your hearts and let the harmony
be under my direction. Songs of sadness and songs of
joy sing to me, for my grief and my delight.

Let me tune your lives to the music of heaven. These
songs without words are songs of my love for you and
your love for me.

Look for every sign of my love. Look for lives
changed, hearts melted, deeds of mercy and kindness,
wounds healed.

Look for sins forgiven. Look for joyful praise. Look for
the sign of the cross.

How I love you! The breadth and depth of my love
you cannot even glimpse. My love is enough to fill not
only the earth but the whole universe.

If it were not for my love all the nations of the earth
would be plunged into darkness and the whole universe
would cease to be.

And yet I love each one of you tenderly. I care for
you, I save you, I heal you. All I ask from you is your
love for me – nothing more and nothing less. Will
you love me and do my will?

The depths of healing love

Through suffering I am breaking and moulding you. Do you think I have let you suffer too much? No, because through suffering I am remaking you in my own image – the image of my glory.

You must accept that you are broken and accept your sin. Why do you try to hide so much? Who will dare to throw a stone at you? All have sinned and fallen short of my glory.

Don't condemn yourself but forgive yourself. Let me heal you and give you my peace.

If you only knew the depths of my healing love! My love is an ocean where your sorrows can be drowned and your sins can be plunged so deep that they are out of reach and taken away.

This water is water of healing. Its salt purifies all your festering wounds and makes them clean.

Float on the surface of the ocean and hear the waves gently lapping around you. Don't contend but be content to let me support you and carry you along.

Don't be afraid, because no harm will come to you. My will is nothing but good.

The offering of the heart

Your duty to me is to love me with joy and gladness so that my love radiates from you like the glow around a candle and attracts those who know their need of me.

Are you continually praising me? Are you continually giving thanks that I speak to you as a friend?

Are you one with me in heart and mind? Is your will submitted to my will? Are you strengthened by my power?

If you want to answer "Yes" to these you are serving me to my glory and I will work through you.

Come to me as you are

"Just as I am" shall be your motto.

"Just as I am" no fabrication, excuses, self-justification, special pleading or leaning.

"Just as I am" means your soul laid bare without trimmings.

"Just as I am" means listen first and speak after. Let your conversation be without guile, pure and simple.

I look on the heart and not on the exterior so come to me in simplicity and don't dissemble. When your heart is set on me I can change you and perfect you.

I am the Lord who knows you as you are and I love you, so don't be afraid. I never turn anyone away but I hold out my arms to welcome you and I come all the way to meet you.

Once you have turned towards me you have nothing more to fear.

For the people of the USSR

Crushed against a wall and trodden under foot are you, my people behind the Iron Curtain, but I will pick you up from the dust and I will heal you and restore you.

I will give you strength to stand firm when hands reach to dash your head against the stones and the boot is raised against you.

I will stay the power of the wicked, and the beauty of my truth will shine like a beacon in the darkness to show my way. Many will see the light of my risen glory and worship me.

My blessing rests upon you because this is my work. The power of my love will do this.

Love one another

Love one another because that is my will. Be kind to one another and prefer others before yourselves.

If someone hurts you, forgive. If someone insults you, forgive. Forgive out of my love for you. Then my love can grow and blossom amongst you and the fruit of my love will be sweet.

How lovely it is when you live together in unity. My Spirit will give you that deep and lovely fellowship that I desire for you. If you love one another like that who can resist my love?

This is the love with which I won the victory over death, the love that paid the price for your redemption. This is the love that loses all but gains all.

Ask me for this love and I will give it to you, my little flock, because I am your good shepherd and I have given my life for you.

A leopard without spots

Change your spots, my leopard. Can a leopard change his spots? No, but I will change you, not just on the outside but in the heart and in the depths of your being.

I will make you live for me. I will change you and perfect you so that you show forth my glory.

You will worship me in heaven without spot or blemish. This is how I see you now – a leopard without spots – because I see in you the perfection which I have given you by my death and resurrection.

I look on you with love, not with condemnation. It is my love which will transform you and change your spots.

Birds of paradise

My fledglings, try your wings and learn to soar near to the heavens. Taste the freedom of the air and learn to rest on the thermals that will carry you and support you as you fly.

As you learn to launch out from the earth where you are held by gravity, your wings will become stronger and you won't fear to fall.

I have given you the freedom of the air to be your element. On your own you can do no more than flutter along the ground, but trust yourselves to me and make the wide heavens your field of operations, a field without horizons, because there is no end to my seeing and doing.

When you are grounded there are many dangers and many things are obscure, but borne aloft by my love, I will show you a pattern of my work and my will, and I will let you encompass the earth without hindrance. When you ask for anything in my name I will give it to you.

You are birds of paradise, fledglings now, but you will inhabit paradise with me. Paradise is your true habitat; there you will know yourselves to be truly at home. Eat the bread of life, my fledglings, and let me strengthen your wings.

On your own you cannot fly, but birds of paradise are made to use their wings.

My love for the Church

My Church, you are my beloved and I delight in you.
Know the love in my heart for you. This is the reason
for my gifts of grace to you. I will give you all you
need and more because I give out of my own
overflowing love.

I give all. Don't bite the hand that feeds you, but take
my gifts with gladness and use them.

There is one gift I require of you – your heart – but
I never demand, I ask. What is this love that asks but
does not demand? It is the love that was obedient even
to death on the cross.

To save you I gave myself. That is my love.
Remember who I am and love me in return.

For my Church whom I love with all my heart I speak
words of love. In my love I speak to my beloved. It is
springtime and the sound of spring songs is in the air.

Come with me, my beloved, and know my love.

In your failure is your success

When will you learn what is for your own good? When will you learn to rest in my peace?

You are pursued by seven hounds, seven fears which will tear you to pieces: fear of being known, fear of knowing yourself, fear of failure, fear of not achieving enough, fear of loneliness, fear of the thoughts and opinions of others, fear of relying on me.

One fear alone will make you whole and that is fear of me. My thoughts are not your thoughts and my ways are not your ways. What is success to you is failure to me.

You succeed when you find me in failure. You succeed when you let me take away your pride. You succeed when you stop trying to activate and let me act instead. You succeed when you rely on me and not on yourself.

The desire to succeed is deeply ingrained in you and so is the desire to please others. Put your hope and trust in me and I myself will bring you to my own perfection – the perfection that is well-pleasing to me.

You are custodians of my goodness

I speak to you, my Church, with love and with sadness. If you knew only the smallest part of my love for you, you would praise me night and day with your whole heart. You would give me your heart as an offering of love and your worldly goods you would place at my feet saying: "Lord, take all that you want and use it to feed the hungry, the hungry in body and in soul."

Do you know how many there are who starve for lack of my word and my truth, whose hearts die for lack of my love? There is a famine in the hearts of men and women, and yet here I stand, waiting to give my richest blessings to least and to greatest.

This is my grief, that my Church, the love of my life, shrugs her shoulders and shades her eyes from the light of my love. You are my chosen ones, but I chose you to serve, first with your hearts, then with your lives, then with all that you possess.

All that you are and all that you have is given by me and you hold it in trust from me. You brought nothing into this world and you will take nothing out.

You are custodians of my goodness, commissioned by me and you must be generous as I am generous to you. I am loving and giving to you. I want you to be loving and giving to me.

That is what I ask. Think on these things.

I will never crush you

I will never crush you. It is your fear that crushes you and the burdens that you bear. I will take away your fear and carry your burdens for you.

How light and glad your hearts will be when you learn to trust me and know my loving kindness. I am your Glorious One who lifts up your head. Hold your heads up high because you are sons and daughters of the Most High.

It is the powers of evil and the rulers of this world who crush and destroy. I save you, I build you up, I comfort you, I support you, I establish you because I love you.

If you think that I would destroy you ask my Spirit to show you my true love. I have proved my love for you by dying on the cross. Look around you and see all the signs of my love, and never doubt that I think of you with compassion and tenderness.

This is not love as you have known it. It is love that loves you for yourself. I came to heal the sick, not the healthy, and my love is poured out for all who are far off so that I can bring them near.

You are afraid because you don't know me. When you know me you will have no more fear. Try me and see.

I am your peace

You need my peace but you don't know where to look. You look in yourselves, you look in the world, you look in silence and withdrawal from the world.

My peace is not there, my peace is in me and I give you my peace by my Spirit. It is he who brings my peace and he who opens your heart to receive my peace.

He fills you with my peace and he keeps you in my peace. Then whether you are alone or in the midst of a crowd, at ease or in hardship, in silence or in clamour, whatever sorrows come or joys, you know my peace deep within you, at an unassailable depth, in the place where I dwell in you.

Then the body of my Church will be like a deep river flowing from the spring of my living water out into the desert of the world, to be a channel of refreshment, to quench the thirst of those who seek for my peace. The desert will blossom like a garden of Paradise and I myself will tend and water it.

In my Father's garden the river of peace makes everything show forth in its true beauty. Flowers and fruits will gladden the heart and satisfy the soul. I myself will walk in the garden in the cool of the evening and my presence will be a blessing beyond compare.

I am your peace and when you know me you know my peace.

Your heart is made for me

I want to be first in your heart, first above all and before all. I am the one through whom everything was created. I am the first cause and the first fruit of all creation, yet I want to be first in your heart, because in your heart I choose to make my dwelling place.

Ask me to come and I will make my home with you. My Holy Spirit will come in and he will unlock the door. Then I will take possession of what is rightfully my own. Your heart is made for me and when I come you know my peace and joy.

Don't reject me. Don't leave me homeless. Don't make me an outcast. Don't leave me alone and unwanted. I will not force an entrance. I am the host but I want to be welcomed as a guest.

When I come in you will hear the sound of music and dancing. There will be a sweet perfume in the air. A fresh breeze will blow through the open windows. A glow of comfort will come from the walls.

A heart that is consecrated to me is like a room that is blessed to my service. It is a house of prayer, a temple of my Holy Spirit. It is built on a rock and it will never be moved but it will stand firm for ever.

Be kind to one another

Kindness, loving kindness, motivated by my love, is a
mark of my grace in you. Be kind to one another and
let others show kindness to you.

I am kind to you all without favour or reserve. My
wonderful kindness to you is like the blue of a fair
day, like the soft rain in the growing season. It is the
touch of one who loves you, the smile of one who cares
for you.

In my kindness there is nothing violent, nothing
abrasive, but I give out my kindness with openhanded
gentleness.

Kindness is at first in your hearts, then in your words
and deeds. Be kind to one another. Be open to give
and receive kindness.

My love is the laughter in your heart

Gaze on my face and see how lovingly I look upon you. My love is the glow of health for you, the sweet pleasure of enjoyment, laughter in the heart, perfect well being. My love makes you come alive; it is new every day.

My love cradles you at each moment of your birth in me and lays you to rest at each moment of your dying for me. So many births and deaths, all blessed by my love, make up your life, and always my love shines upon you.

Truly, truly, I say, I love you. Go to the furthest parts of the universe, distances beyond your mind to conceive, and my love will be there.

This is the love I offer you. This is my gift to you. This is what your heart seeks to know. This is the stability of your soul.

My love will burn beyond a thousand ages, and when your life is hidden in me you will know the love I speak of because you will know me.

Latch-key children

You are like latch-key children. There is no incentive to come home because you think there is no one on the other side of the door. If the house is empty it is better to roam the streets and pick up company.

Try the door; there is no need to use a key. I will open it wide for you and welcome you with a loving embrace. The rooms are warm, the food is on the table, fresh flowers scent the air.

This is the place of your comfort and rest. Come in to me and I will talk with you. This is where you belong. This is my presence.

A call to repentance

Repent because you have trodden my glory underfoot.
You presume upon my patience and you have
forgotten that I am holy.

You take my love but you don't give me yours. You
say I am the Christ but you won't suffer for me.

I am your glory but you seek the glory of the world. I
count for nothing when you disobey me, but I will be
exalted over all the earth when I come in glory.

Angels will spread my light on either side. Then you
will say I am the Most High. Then you will kneel
before my Sovereign Grace and you will lift me up
with your praise. My holy name will be on your lips,
and my holy will will be written in your hearts for
evermore. You will be mine as I am yours.

Come to be now and let my glory shine in you. Let
praises resound to my glory in your hearts and in your
lives, in my Church and in the world.

There is no need to fear because I love you. Don't
hold me at arm's length but come close. Don't keep
your distance but come. Aren't I more to you than
husband, wife or children? Isn't my glory more than
the pale reflections you see on earth?

How afraid you are!

How afraid you are! Don't be afraid. I am your
friend, your husband. I am your strength and support.
I am your salvation and your song.

I am your joy and your delight. I am the one who
always loves you. I am always faithful.

I am your eternal good. I am your praise for
evermore. You will always be mine and I will never let
you go.

I made you for myself, and without me you are like a
widow who mourns the loss of her loved one. Without
me you will know only the desolation of loneliness.

Come to me and know the fellowship of my love.
Come to me and do not be afraid.

You are not a puppet on a string

I will not manipulate you. You are not like a puppet on a string

I have given you life – given – because you are free of your Maker. Your life that belonged to me belongs to you, to be given back to me as an offering of the love in your heart.

I have made you free, and the cords which bind you to me and to each other must be tied with your own hands.

I will show you and teach you and enable you, but it is your choice and your decision.

From Holy Russia my holiness will shine forth

Mix your glad voices with the cries of my hungry
people and never forget that both come to my ears and
move my heart of love.

From despotism and from oppression deliver my
people by your prayers and your love. Pray for my
people behind the Iron Curtain; deliver them from the
desolation of evil. By the power of my Spirit the
curtain can be torn in two, and from Holy Russia my
holiness will shine forth.

I am the treasure in the hearts of my faithful people,
and by their obedience to me they will show forth my
glory in the world. When evil seems to close on every
side, and my people are suffocated in a strait-jacket,
my glory will transfigure the body of my Church
behind the Iron Curtain, and the power of my love
will move your hearts to cry: ''Blessed Jesus! You are
Lord Most High!''

I love all my people, but those who are persecuted for
me are the gems in my diadem. Those who are
steadfast in their love for me against all the powers of
evil will have the place of honour in my kingdom.

Love me with that steadfast love before destruction
comes, and then you will be ready to withstand the
evil of the days to come. I am your strength and your
only refuge and I want to be first in your hearts, now
and always.

The two faces of faith

Which face of faith are you seeking: the acceptable face or the unacceptable face?

The acceptable face is the one that makes no demands and demands no sacrifice.

The unacceptable face is my face, spattered by blood from a crown of thorns.

The acceptable face of faith bears no scar because it is buried in the sand, but the unacceptable face is bruised and wounded. That face shines with the light of my love and is covered in my glory.

Seek my face and seek my glory.

Tethered to a stake?

When you are like a goat tethered to a stake, however lush the grass around you, you have lost your freedom.

When you can't see further than a circle around your feet, you may think you have happiness on that spot, but lift your eyes and see the distant hills, and you will long to be free.

When your eyes have seen the glory of the Lord, you will mourn the rope that holds you. You need to be free to tramp where I lead you.

When I call you to follow me I will cut through the rope, and though the grass may be thin and the way stony, I myself will be your companion, and my fellowship will gladden your heart.

My peace will be like a velvet path, and you will have no need of a map because you will have my hand to guide you.

Cupful upon cupful

Crystal clear is the deep well from which my living water flows. It is pure with the strong purity of my Spirit. There is no trace of any impurity to cloud its brightness.

Come, let me immerse you in my living water. I will cleanse you and restore you. Here your soul can drink and never thirst again.

What can you do to gain this living water? Only come and ask me. This water of life is mine to give. I will pour it out freely for you, cupful overflowing upon cupful.

This is living water from the living God, who pours out his Spirit upon all his people without favour and without stint.

The remedy for your dryness is the fresh water of my Spirit. This is sweet water, glinting in the sunlight. Here you will come to no harm. Come, drink for your soul's good.

A callus on the heart?

Calluses on your feet are made when your skin rubs
against ill-fitting shoes. Calluses in you heart are made
when you rub against your own ill-fitting will.

My will is perfect for you, perfect fitting and perfect in
loveliness. Don't be misled by outward appearances
but trust that my will is exactly right for you.

My will is the only true comfort for you. If you don't
put on my will but put on your own will, at first you
won't notice the damage to your heart, but then you
will begin to feel the pain.

Put yourself in my hands and let me choose what is
fitting for you, because my Spirit is your heart's true
Comforter, and I will choose for you what you most
need.

My time is now

My patience is active patience, not passive patience. In my patience is all the strength of my love and my deep longing for your well-being.

My time is always now. At every moment of every day my time is now. In every age throughout eternity my time is now.

In direct opposition to your inclinations I want to turn you round to face me now. Who are you to say to the Lord of your life: "I will attend to my own business first and then I will consider your claims"?

Would you insult your Maker and harden your hearts against your Redeemer? The whole of my love for you is overflowing upon you now. I have not waited to pour out my love for you. How long will you withhold your love from me?

Jesus is Lord

Mouthing words across an abyss won't be an effective
way of making your message heard. Lift up your voice
and shout! Direct the sound forward by putting your
hands to your mouth. Several voices together are
better than one, and many voices will be clearly heard.

If my people will speak together of what I have done,
if many voices are raised in praise of me, there will be
a joyful sound that will carry across the divide.

Shout the acclamation: "Jesus is Lord!" and the
mountains will take up the echo, and the valleys will
ring with the call to worship me.

My Church, don't be afraid to speak my truth. Let
my voice sound out through you.

Love for one another

Listen to me and fill your hearts with love and mercy for each other. My love which flows, world without end, in the burning fire of my Spirit, can overflow in your hearts and purify you from all your pride and bitterness.

Where you have my love you will have love for one another. If you have no love for one another, my love is not there.

Open your hearts to me. It is my love that will shine through you, my love and only my love. Where you see deeds of love and mercy, that is my love. Where you see grace and truth, that is my love. Where you see the beauty of holiness, that is my love.

Where you see kindness and courtesy of heart, that is my love. Where you see faithfulness and perseverance, that is my love. Where you see humility and willingness to suffer, that is my love.

Be open to each other as you are open to me. Let my love penetrate and permeate your lives so that all your thoughts and words and deeds are redeemed by me.

Seek me in silence

Flashing lights and peals of thunder strike terror into
the heart, but my still small voice that speaks to you in
your heart is the voice of one who loves you and who
cherishes you as his own.

Listen to the voice of your Redeemer and hear my call
to you. Don't fill your life with clamour but seek me
in silence and in the deep quiet of stillness.

I will come to you, I will be with you and I will show
myself to you. I am your vision and your inspiration,
and your fellowship with me will be sweet.

Trust yourself to the open water

Pray that my life in you will be renewed. Pray that my Spirit will enliven your hearts with the breath of my life. Pray for my life-giving love. I will give you new life, my Church, but you must understand that your life is in me.

O, keep your hearts set on me, like a sail that is set to catch the wind. Don't pull on the oars but let my power move you. Be open to me and I will fill you with my power.

You will cut through the water with ease; you will not be becalmed. The peace of a backwater is deceptive: it is stagnant and the overhanging branches shelter you from the breeze.

If you trust yourself to me in the open water, you will feel a surge of power, and a spirit of adventure will call you to explore unknown reaches.

Commit your life to me and let me fill you with my life.

My kingdom is conceived in prayer

Governments and principalities and powers will topple
and fall in the dust, but my kingdom is an everlasting
kingdom because my love and my power are
everlasting.

The kingdoms of this world are like towers built with
wooden bricks by a child. When he grows tired of his
game he knocks them over and no one mourns that
they are gone. Lightheartedly he tosses the bricks into
a box, and the work of an hour is forgotten in less
than a minute.

My kingdom is like a picture that is painted, an icon,
conceived in prayer, executed in prayer and reverenced
in prayer.

My kingdom is green and gold; green because it grows
and flourishes, and gold for the glory that is mine.

My kingdom is my will, loved and obeyed. If you love
me and obey my will you are citizens of my everlasting
kingdom.

Let me arrange the stitches

Your life is like a sampler embroidered by me. Let me arrange the stitches to show my skill. Let me choose the colours to blend together and to please the eye.

Let me finish the work I have started. I shall never grow tired of the work of my hand. Learn to understand and admire the beauty and symmetry of my design.

Let the text sink into your heart: "As in Adam all die, even so in Christ shall all be made alive." Point all who look at you towards me.

As more of my design is made visible, murmurs of delight will increase to shouts of praise and adoration because everything that I make is very good and the flaws that mar your life now, I will remove and replace with my perfection.

The task I am giving you

The task I am giving you is to pray – to pray and yet
again to pray. This is the work that I set before you
and this is how you join your will with mine.

Pray that my kingdom will come, that my goodness
will be known, that my glory will be praised.

Pray that my will will be done, first in your hearts,
then in my Church, then in the world.

Pray that my people will know that they belong to me.
Pray that in the world my love and my truth will
convince many hearts that I am the Lord. Pray that
your faith may be firm to look for the fulfilment of my
promises.

Watch and pray. Stay awake and pray. Pray with me.
Join your hearts to the endless intercession I make for
all peoples.

You hold them in your hearts through me and I hold
them in my heart through you.

This is the work of love and prayer I give you.

Let us dance together

Dance for me in your heart. Dance to the music of the joy I give you. While you are still young dance for me.

Move your body to the rhythm that I give you. Learn the steps I teach you. Let my Spirit be the spirit of the dance in you.

Leap and let me lift you up in the exhilaration of knowing me. Let me show you how to dance to the lovesong that I sing to you. I love to see you dance.

I will give you a new dance to suit your beauty, and the longing that is in you will reach out to me.

Let us dance together, you and I. See! The beat of your heart matches the beat of the music of heaven.

A message for Sunday

Sunday is your day of rest when I invite you to a celebration of love at my house. Come and eat with me at my table. Come and praise me for my never-ceasing care for you. Come and give thanks to me for my great goodness. Come and worship me. Tell me that all that you are is mine.

I invite you to come together to share your faith and your love: stand together and build together a community of faith and love. Rejoice in the One who saves and is alive amongst you. Receive new life and new light. Receive the comfort and strength of my Holy Spirit. Know me for yourselves and make me known.

Let every Sunday be a day of celebration, a resurrection festival, a day of joy – joy in my victory and my power, my glory and my triumph.

Gilding the lily

Gilding the lily gives to the lily the appearance of what it is not. Instead of the soft bloom of the petals there is hardness encrusted on; instead of the purity of spotless white which rests the eyes, there is a brash yellow harshness; instead of cool smoothness there is a rough patina that masks the natural beauty.

I have given you the beauty of my own Spirit. It is natural because I bestow it. Don't cover my godliness with worldliness. I have made you as you are because it pleases me.

I look at the beauty of the heart, and the heart that is open to me is like a lily that is reaching out in openness to me. The lilies that adorn my sanctuary are the open hearts of my people. This beauty that I give will never fade, but the fresh dew of my Spirit will keep the bloom of everlasting youth upon you.

Many have dreamed of finding the elixir of life. My life in you never grows old, but my Spirit renews in you the succulence of a fresh flower that gives glory to me.

Nothing that is of the world is arrayed like this, perfect in love and purity.

Wave after wave will come over you

Grant me free access to every part of your life. My Spirit is like a tide which comes in and finds its way into every corner and crevice in the rocks, washing round them and submerging them. This water is salt water for purification, and it makes the rough places smooth.

This is the work of many years. Your whole lifetime is the time given to you to be changed by me.

Every day of your life, all day and every day, open your whole self to me. Wave after wave of the ocean of my Spirit will come over you, like the gentle waves lapping or like the breakers crashing and throwing spray high into the air.

The action of water upon rocks is imperceptible but sure. This must be your prayer: "Come to me, break into me, flood me, purify me, smooth me."

I am your praise and your joy

When, in your heart, you know that my joy is making you glad, go forth in confidence and tell of me, giving praise to me. Exult in what I have done and what I am doing. Speak in my name and praise my holy name.

When your heart leaps within you, let your voice proclaim my good news because I am the living Word and I am made flesh in you. "I am your God. I have saved you because I love you. You will live with me for ever because you are mine." This is my word for all humanity.

I am your praise and your joy. Joy overflowing will lift your heart as you hope in me.

The joy that I give you is the exultation of heaven. It is as if a dancer could leap from the ground high over the heads of the people watching. It is as if a singer could extend her range by two octaves.

It is as if a single violin could play with the notes of a double bass, a 'cello and a viola as well. It is as if a man could fly near to the sun without melting his wings.

This is the joy I give you by my Spirit, joy that defies circumstances, that depends only on knowing me.

Joy in my love

Joy, joy, joy comes into your heart when you know my love. This is the joy of heaven. It is the joy of being in me and I in you. It is the joy of being at one with me and with my people. It is the joy I give my Church, my bride, in whom is all my joy.

This joy is in the rightness of all things – my promise to you. It is the joy of my goodness which is in all my creation because I made it very good.

Above all it is joy in my love because I have loved and saved everything that I have made, and everything that is in my hands will come at last to be one in my love.

Joy, joy, joy will fill your hearts on that day because my love will be your all, and all you who love me will be filled with the joy of my love for evermore.

Rejoice now in the hope I have given you and my promise that your joy will be fulfilled.

The love that holds you

Are you holding steadfastly to my loving purposes for
you? Do you come with confidence to the throne of
grace? Do you know the love with which I cherish
you, that tender love full of compassionate kindness,
the love that saves and heals?

There is no love like my love because all love comes
from me. I am love itself and when I give my love I
give myself.

What is my love like? It is a rose that blooms for ever,
soft and fresh; it is the blood of the martyrs and
mother's milk.

It is the comfort of one who always welcomes you; it is
the lustre of a priceless pearl; it is sparkling spring
water for someone who is dying of thirst.

It is the rich earth, the ground of your being because
you are rooted in love; it is the greatest grace and it is
for all people so that all shall be contained in my love
and all shall be surpassingly well.

Don't misconstrue my purposes for you. They are all
for good, for your best good.

Don't be afraid, but come with joyful eagerness to the
love that holds you gently but will never let you go.

Be taught by me to mourn your pride

I will teach you to mourn your pride. I will teach you, in your inmost being, to be conscious only of me, and to know that it is my power working in you – my power alone – that accomplishes my will.

Ask for the grace that my Spirit gives to humble yourself before me. It is through the heart that is humble and open before me that I can do great things.

If you think you stand you will fall, but if you humble yourself I will raise you up.

This is what it is to be humble: it is to know that I have made you according to my will and my desire because it pleases me.

It is to know that all that you are is given by me and belongs to me. It is to know my power working in you and my Spirit's gifts enabling you.

It is to give thanks to me and praise my holy name. It is to rest content with what I have given and what I will give because all that you need I will fulfil.

To be humble is to worship me in faith and love, looking always to me to guide you and support you.

To be humble is to know yourself as my beloved, one with all those I have saved, one with all peoples for whom I have poured out my love.

It is done and you will see it

Fanciful and fearful dreams and portents, anxious thoughts and bitterness of heart are the roots of sorrow and disintegration in your lives.

Let your love be rooted in me. Fix your eyes upon me. Find in me your true and lasting peace. I am a secure anchor for you, a safe harbour. I am an overhanging rock beneath which you can shelter.

I am the one who runs to pick you up when you fall. My arms embrace you to give you comfort and hope. Trust yourself to me. Let me kiss your hand as a mother kisses her wounded child. Let me speak words of endearment to soothe you and words of encouragement to set you on your feet.

I will do this for you because my love is purer than any mother's love. Were you afraid to tell your mother of your secret woes? Don't be afraid of me. I know the depths of your heart already. Is there anything in you that I don't know? My word is the truth: I love you.

Therefore be joyful in my love whatever befalls you.

My glorious love is the foundation of the earth, and because all goodness comes from me I have already raised you from earth to heaven.

It is done and you will see it. Disease and destruction and detriment I have carried away on my cross. Now it is all health and heart's ease and help, and so you must rejoice.

What rebellion is this?

Will you come all the way with me? Why are you so
reluctant to follow? You come a little way along the
path and then you lag behind.

Will you come to the top of the mountain and over the
top with me? What is so good about coming half-way?
Why are you so lukewarm? You are neither hot nor
cold, neither coming nor going, neither a bright flame
burning, nor a blackened ember.

You are neither full nor empty. You neither worship
me with your whole heart nor do you forget me quite.

Have you not heard? I am a God of excesses. I want
your whole heart, not part of it. I have given to you
my overflowing love without stint, pressed down,
running over, a deluge, a pillar of fire burning for
ever.

My goodness is a harvest of superabundance. I am a
God of too much, more than enough. My blessings I
multiply. My glory is without end.

By birth and by new birth you belong to me. What
rebellion is this that you want to walk alone? I made
you to walk beside me and to go where I shall lead
you. I have implanted in you my character and I have
imprinted upon your heart the marks of my nails.

You think it is a stigma to be seen with me. You are
ashamed of me. In truth, my stigmata are given to
those who are not careful to preserve their lives, but
have given their lives to me.

As a swan in beauty and grace

Be to me, in beauty and in grace, like a swan. In the morning, in the evening, by day and by night, glide trustingly on the still waters of my Spirit.

The life that is based on prayer in me is like the water that has no ruffled surface but a smooth peace that reflects the glory of the heavens above.

Let me support you as the water supports the light body of the swan. Let the current of my love draw you gently downstream.

Be always in prayer. You are made to pray as the swan is made to float and fly. Water and air are your elements because my Spirit is the element in which you were baptized.

I love your beauty and grace, my Church. What a mastery of effortless grace I can give you! Don't strive. Only trust yourselves to me.

Who teaches the swan her beauty and grace, and who gives her feathers of the purest white? It is your Lord, who can surely do the same for you.

I am in mind and in matter

Mind over matter is not my truth. I am in mind and in matter. I am Spirit and truth. Will you lose your life to gain it? Will you let me live in you? You are a temple of my Holy Spirit, so you are made holy, body and soul, by me.

I want you to love me with your whole self, to give your whole self into my control. What you do with your nail parings matters to me. Aren't they matter created by me? Haven't they clothed hands raised up in prayer, hands that served those I love?

You are to be submitted, body and soul, to me. You are to be a living sacrifice to give joy to me.

You are to recognize my gifts, and with your hands you are to build my temple not made with hands. When my Spirit lives in you, you become body, mind and spirit, one in me.

No part of your life is outside my life. Mind and matter are consecrated by me.

A tidal wave of love

Fill your hearts with my love. My love is like a tidal wave that has covered the whole earth. It is a flood of blessing, not of judgement. Let my love overflow in your hearts so that I can bless others through you.

My Church is a fountain of blessings for all the world. Blessed are you, my Church, and blessed is the work of your hands if you do it for love of me.

Let me show you those whose hearts are in need. They are standing knee-deep in water splashing down from my fountain. But they are deluded. They think it is a brood of vipers tangled about their legs and they are afraid. Poor, sad hearts that cannot tell the difference. Teach them to look at the Source of the fountain that leaps in the air. Help them to open their eyes and see that there are no vipers but only streams of living water.

This water will wash away disease and make the skin like that of a little child. Once they have seen that it is clean and clear, teach them to plunge in and be healed.

Rivers of love flow out of my heart for the dry parched deserts of the world. What drought you have suffered!

My Church, how can you find this water if you have lost the art of divining? To find the divine water, let my fountain flow freely amongst you and I will make you a blessing to the world.

The wideness of my mercy

My name is above all names most worthy of honour and praise. My nature is to love, to give, to save, to forgive. It is my love that is above all things most wonderful.

O my Church, how you need to know my love in your hearts, so that you may be my heart of love for all humanity.

This is your work because I brought you to birth to give my life to the earth. I love all peoples and all nations. I have died to save them all. When will you understand the largeness of my love and the wideness of my mercy?

The whole earth is held in my arms as I hang on the cross. My love includes – it does not exclude. My love is so tender and compassionate for each one of my children. My love is so far above what you know of my love.

Your hearts are like peanuts, but even out of peanuts may come the oil of compassion. Let my Spirit press you and release the oil so that I may bless the world through you.

Colour is my gift to a dull world

Give such a colourful account of my love that those
who listen are attracted by all those warm hues. Let
your actions speak of my brightness, and your deeds
portray my glowing sunstar, with its rosy rays that
light up the sky as far as the horizon.

A good deed from a loving heart shines into eternity,
and those who come near to me reflect the light of my
love to those who are far away.

Colour and radiance are my gifts to a dull world: I am
the splendour of heaven seen on earth. O that your
hearts might learn to love ever more deeply! A little
tint will deepen into a glorious fullness of crimson and
scarlet and burnished gold.

The beauty of good deeds, by their warm colours,
arrests the attention, and what was monochrome can
become a bright tapestry, hanging down from heaven
to earth, designed by a Master Craftsman, alive with
the vivid hues of his heart and mind, embroidered on
the canvas by a thousand hands which have learnt to
weave the colours in a school of obedience.

It is a sunburst of life and light. The centre is dark
and deep, like a blood-red sun, bringing a new dawn
to rise over the world, like the promise of love, like the
agony of a darkened soul healed by the touch of my
Spirit, like a rose without a thorn.

I will grip you kindly but firmly

Reach out to me and take my hand which is already stretched out towards you. I will grip you kindly but firmly. I will pull you from the treacherous bog on to dry ground where you can tread safely.

When you are trying to pick your way through the mire, and every tussock gives way into water and slime, when the darkness is falling and night is coming on, when your heart is heavy and your spirit sinks, call out for me and I will come to you.

The comfort I bring you is my glad presence. A hundred footsore travellers I can house for the night. Come and join in the singing and make merry with psalms and hymns.

The joy of fellowship will fill you with enough strength to suffer patiently and to continue the hard way in the morning. Every step you take brings you nearer to the heavenly country, and I am with you all the way.

You are creatures of beauty and gladness

When you come before me leave behind you all those
ties of resentment and unforgiveness that hold you
down. Shed them as a caterpillar sheds its skin in
order to grow. I ask you to look back in love, and I
want you to look forward to the glory that I will give
you.

When you come to faith in me, you are like a butterfly
that emerges from a chrysalis. You are clothed in the
vibrant colours of the new life I give you. You are
adorned with the patterns of heaven, a perfect
symmetry that mirrors the perfection of my kingdom.

Light and bright on the wing, sucking nectar in
stillness, inhabiting the air, you are creatures of beauty
and gladness.

As a caterpillar knows only its own life and its own
ways, and does not imagine the splendour of
metamorphosis that will be accomplished, so you do
not know what you will be, but I have given you
hope: you will be changed in the twinkling of an eye.
You will be fit for heaven by my doing. By my death
and resurrection you are creatures that dwell in
eternity, made gorgeous by my giving.

Mercy breaks the barriers of the human heart

Live my life in obedience to my Spirit. In my love go on to love.

In mercy show mercy to those who know no mercy in their hearts. What will break down the barriers of the human heart but my love and my mercy, against which the gates of hell shall not prevail?

Love and mercy are like the action of an underground river on limestone, wearing it away over the years, making a channel to flow out over a hillside.

Love and mercy have no source but in me. When you let my love and mercy seep through you, you are like a stalactite that grows slowly and surely. Every particle bonds to another, to make a formation reaching down to the ground where others are being built up to meet you. Many will link and merge to make a strong pillar from ground to ceiling, a solid creation that was not there before.

Over time I will make a gallery of grandeur where each tiny particle has played its part. Though you do not now see the endless structure which is the work of my hands, let love and mercy flow underground and overground so that, seen and unseen, I can continue what I have begun.

The tears of all creation

Come to me, all who are sad and weary. Come, all
who are stricken with disease. Come to me, all who
are suffering and in pain, all who are maimed by strife
and warfare, all who are hurt in your hearts, all who
are killed before you are born, all who are struck down
in your prime, all who live desolate in the waste lands
of the world.

Come to me and I will come to you. I will wipe away
all your tears.

Without me your tears would be a deluge, a flood
covering the face of the earth, drowning all the world
in an ocean of deep sorrow. How could anyone live?
How could anyone smile again?

Hope in me. Hope in the man of sorrows who is
acquainted with grief. My Spirit is the dove of peace,
promising the safety of the whole earth.

My Church is the ark for the gathering in of all
peoples. From my side, the gushing stream of water
contains the tears of all creation, a mighty torrent that
flows through heaven itself, and gives life to the new
Jerusalem, the heavenly city.

Not one tear that you have shed has sunk into the
earth to be wasted, but I have collected your tears in
my bottle because they are precious to me. I will
remember them all.

Pilgrims on the march

Move, as if with wings or on crutches, the fit and the fleet, the halt and the lame. Move, but don't stand still.

All who are making their way into my kingdom are moving towards me. Some are being carried on stretchers, some are running ahead, bearing torches to light the way.

There is no mechanical transport. This is park and walk. As you come into the world so you will go out. Babies are carried in arms, toddlers on shoulders. Some with joy are dancing, others are stumbling, faint and weary. The old are steadied and supported, and no one is ever left behind.

All this crowd of people is streaming from the four corners of the world. They are those who have heard me calling; they have seen the glimmer of a new light in the sky. One beckons another.

These are not strangers but pilgrims, all going the same way. Their greeting is: "The peace of the Lord be with you." They seek the kingdom that will never end. They help each other, and each considers his brothers and sisters better than himself.

They are learning obedience through suffering, and the fellowship of my Spirit is with them. They will sit down at my table in my kingdom and feast with the King of kings.

I am the expert gardener

Be assured of my loving mercy and my power to
change your hearts. I reach down to the root of sin
and pluck it out. I sow the seeds of my goodness and
holiness.

I see the shoot appear. I tend and water the plant as it
grows. I can make a whole garden of grace in your
hearts, an abundance of scent and colour to give joy to
me.

When the ground is sterile and polluted with
weedkiller, and the first plants wither and die, I will
not give up. I will take away the poor soil and lay
down good soil.

I will sow more seeds and more, until at last some
begin to grow. I will make a garden that will give
glory to me. I am the expert gardener and I know how
to make your garden grow. I will provide the sunshine
and the gentle showers.

I will take away from your hearts the love of self, the
fear of others, all that is negative and all that opposes
me, all that seeks security in enclosure, and I will
make myself known to you in my love and mercy so
that my power rules your lives.

Then where there were notices up saying: "No entry",
I will come in and you will welcome me. Then your
gardens will be a solace to many who will find me
walking with them in the evening time.

A story without end

My love is like a story without an end. Every chapter
reveals new exploits and new delights of love. The
pages are illuminated with designs of blue and red and
gold – Mary's colours. Every episode tells of my
steadfast love; through every event my love is
manifest.

How faithfully the beloved one awaits the return of the
bridegroom. How she longs to give herself with
abandon to him. With what delicate trust she expects
the denouement.

With a sweet smile of love she looks for him. His
character gives rise to no doubts. She will live happily
ever after when he comes, whose love is already
known. His promise is in her heart. His name is on
her lips. "Come, Lord Jesus", she says, and no
shadows pass across her face.

My love is steadfast love. There is no need to fear,
though the earth be shaken and the nations torn apart;
though the colours become sombre and the gold turns
to black; though a hundred riderless horses charge
across the page, and loathsome creatures, grinning,
twine themselves around the capitals. This is not the
end of the story.

The bridegroom will come and there will be a feast
with laughter and dancing. Then the love which had
never dimmed will be unveiled. The secrets of every
heart will be laid bare, and in my magnificence, the
full story of your Lord's love will be made known.

I want my Church to be one

I want my Church to be one. If you are one with my will you will be one with each other.

I am one with the Father, and when I showed myself to be one with his will I laid down my life in obedience to him upon the cross. I died in oneness with God the Father so that you might be at one with him and with each other.

All who acknowledge me as Saviour of the world are one in me. All who venerate my cross must bear the sacrifice of my cross in their own lives.

My Church must be a seeking community, a growing community, a living community, reaching out in openness together to me. Be teachable, be hungry for my living word, be always on the move and never at a standstill.

Let my Spirit transform you into the visible image of my kingdom, where vested interests and individual prejudices are sacrificed to the common good which is my goodness towards you, conceived, given and poured out by my Spirit on all humanity.

It is *my* beloved Church. You do not belong to yourselves. Ask what is my will, what pleases me, what gives glory to me and I will lead you in my way, I will teach you my truth, I will put my life within you. Then your desire to be one will be my own desire and I will bring it about.

Unity with variety

My Church, as a young man rejoices in the many different expressions of love and affirmation that he receives from his bride as he makes known his love for her, so I rejoice in your infinite variety.

All the expressions of my Church, all the expressions of each heart, are precious to me. In all that you do, affirm me, exalt me, worship me, adore me, submit to me, melt into oneness with me.

Let me cherish every part of my Church. Learn from each other and value each other as I value you.

No part of my Church is a monopoly – my Church is universal.

You are to have unity with variety and to respect what your brothers and sisters have seen of me. Why are you so afraid of what I have shown to them? I have also shown myself to you. I have no favourites. In the whole earth, in all my creation, throughout all time, in all cultures and languages, in all the parts of my Church, I have no favourites.

I have made an infinite variety of faces, I have made an infinite variety of personalities, in each personality and heart I have made infinite variety, and yet by my one perfect and sufficient sacrifice for the sins of the whole world I have made you one in me.

This is unity with variety. This is my call to you, my Church, in this age.

All is held together in me

Glad are my servants who come into my presence with faith and loving trust. If you know me you will have life in death, peace in war, joy in sorrow, hope in uncertainty. Where I am, all these are together.

My heart is in the shape of a tear and there are tears of sorrow and tears of joy. So in me there is profit and loss. I hold together holiness and love, righteousness and compassion, justice and mercy. They are all one in me.

Power and meekness are mine at the same time. Everything that is done is done by me, and everything that is done is done to me. I am the subject and the object, the mover and the moved.

I am the giver of life and the one who suffers death. I am before all time and I am he who came under the yoke of time. I am Spirit and flesh. I am not either–or, but both–and.

From Jerusalem will I reign

O all you peoples of the earth, I have died to save you all.

Through my Church I am calling you to come into my everlasting kingdom. I am making ready a place for you, a place of peace and security, a place of justice. I am coming to bring you home.

When you see me descending in glory, know that I have come to save the whole earth. I have not come in anger, but in love to save you. The grapes of wrath have been destroyed and now I have come to give you a new Passover from heaven.

You shall consume wind and fire. When the earth is devastated, laid waste and bare, I will fill you with my heart's love and the energy of my Spirit.

I have ordained that this mountain on which my throne is set, this rock of resurrection and resplendent glory, this holy place in the holy city of Jerusalem, will be the seat of my authority. From this place will go forth my commands which are full of truth and wisdom.

I am Jesus the mighty warrior, come to rule my kingdom. Be glad, all peoples of the earth, for your King has come.

Turn to me. Look towards Jerusalem, for there your salvation will be revealed. Grace and glory are my garments, and my crown is set with jewels from every nation of the earth.

My love is the light of your life

Will you come along unknown paths with me – paths unknown to you but not to me.

I will lead you. I will pick you up and carry you. As a father encourages his little child I will encourage you, and when you run and skip ahead, I will watch over you to keep you safe. When you are hurt and injured I will care for you, and when you are sick I will stay by your bedside.

There is no moment of your life when I am not loving you to the uttermost. My love is the light of your life in sickness and in health. My touch is the touch of a friend who always wants your good, and always speaks good of you, you whom I have made for fellowship with me.

Trust me by day and by night. Trust the one who is your light and your life, for you have light and life in no other.

Listen to me

Listen to me and not to your own unruly will. Listen to me with your heart and I will give you a sweet and saving knowledge of me.

I have never said: "You will not be buffeted by the world", but only, "Your peace is in me." Love me, and in that love I will give you knowledge that is as different from the knowledge of the world as spring is from winter.

All that is negative and destructive I will redeem. All that is profitable for your learning, all that is life for you, I will teach you in your heart if you come to me in simplicity, like a little child.

I will teach you the only name in heaven and earth by which you may be saved, and I will teach you that love is above all – your love for me and for all those whom I love. I will teach you to put your whole trust in me for yourself and for those you love.

I alone can change your heart and I alone can change the hearts of others.

Faith is God's gift

Faith is of me and of no other. Because I am the living God and faith is my gift, faith gives life to my people. You cannot have life without faith, and from faith comes knowledge of me.

Faith is like a seed blown into a cleft in a rock, growing in adversity. There are few particles of soil, there is little shelter from the storm, but a plant takes root. Come back years later and a colony is established, where once the rocks were bare and bleak.

Faith is like an oasis in the desert, a place of refreshment for travellers who rejoice because the water is a reality and not a mirage.

Finding faith is like finding the path that leads homeward as the night is falling; it is like looking into the face of a friend. It is carrying the cross of the Saviour; it is staying with him world without end.

In knowing yourself you know me

First find me in your own heart and then I will teach you to find me in your brothers and sisters and in all creation.

I am not far away so that you should say, "I cannot reach him. I cannot go there", but I am closer than sinew to bone, closer than breath within you, closer than a lover.

I am Spirit and I dwell in eternity. When I come into your heart I fill every part of your being. I break apart the earthen vessel which held you. Like fermenting wine I cannot be contained.

I am in you to help you to know yourself, for it is in knowing yourself that you know me.

It is not possible to know what is yourself and what is me, for I am in you and you are in me, I am you and you are me. What is eternal has chosen to live within the limits of time, and what was confined within time has become eternal.

Look into your own heart to find me. Search diligently and you will come to the place where I am born anew in you. This incarnation clothes you with majesty divine. I am in you reconciling you to yourself.

The more you look inward, the more you can look outward. As you are reconciled to yourself you will be reconciled to your neighbour.

You who were made in my image are not strangers to me. The breath of my Spirit is in you, and desire for me is in your hearts.

The fire without which you are dead

Close and very close I will hold you, so that you can feel the warmth of my breath, so that the love that burns in my heart for you will warm you through and through.

The ardent love that I have for you burns like tongues of fire upon my breast. Flames rise, crimson and scarlet, orange and gold, a bank, a wall of fire.

To envelop you in this love is my desire. This is the love that says: "Neither do I condemn you", that says: "Your sins are forgiven. Grace and peace to you."

Since I have given all for you I have made you free to love me. I have given you peace, sweet peace, so that in your heart the flames of my love may be kindled from the fire that never burns low.

It is the meek heart that seeks me with due reverence that I will enter. I, who dwell in every human heart, will, by invitation, invade the root of your being. I will burn deep within you, and my searing love will cauterize your imperfection.

So this fire is sweet delight and heart's bane; it is all love and all pain. It is the death and life of self. It is fire without which you are dead.

It is a holy love that burns with the brightness of my truth. Fire surrounds my head like the mane of a lion, like the flames that blaze around the outline of a sun. I am head and heart aflame with truth and love. This is my eternal merit.

When you take me it is I who take you

Take me into your hearts. As a drop of rain falls into a pool and becomes one with it, indistinguishable from it, so when you take me it is I who take you.

Where has the raindrop come from? What is it but vapour condensed from water upon the surface of the earth? So all that you are is of me, part of the cycle of my giving, of my transforming power. What is of me, when it comes back to me, keeps on being transformed into my likeness.

You must lose yourself in me as a raindrop loses itself in a pool. No one, looking at a pool, says that it is made up of thousands of drops of water. He sees the pool's fresh depths and the peace of its smooth surface, the glimmer of fish moving amongst the weed, and the glint of blue and green dragonflies darting above the reeds.

Yet if the raindrops cease to fall the pool dries up, and the fish and the dragonflies are no more. In the same way I have made myself dependent upon your obedience. Whenever you are willing to take me I will take you into myself, but I have made you and saved you and called you and kept you. If you are obedient I have made you so.

You are as free as a raindrop but no freer. Only when a raindrop falls to earth can it do the work it was ordained to do, and it can fall no other way.

I am a God of variety

With artistry an arrangement of flowers is made for a
wedding: pink roses and carnations and foliage fresh
and green. To my glory each is placed, creating
something that not one could be alone.

Each is part of a whole which is greater far and
different in kind from itself. Each flower has a life of
its own, a heart dancing with the joy of life. Each leaf,
cool and green, is a place of peace, resting the eye,
drawing attention to the flowers, filling out the spaces,
leading outwards and back towards the centre.

If you remove one flower there will be a lack; what
was complete will be incomplete. If even one leaf falls
away, the pattern will be distorted from the vision of
the artist.

When you delight in the variety of shades, in the
contrast between flowers and foliage, in the mastery of
shape, texture, colour and design, you are pleased
because each is in its right place.

The carnation does not say to the rose: "Why aren't
you a carnation?" nor do the leaves say: "It would be
better if there were no flowers." Each is what it is
ordained to be, and has been chosen for what it is.
Each enhances the others, and together they are a new
creation.

Your work is to build up the body of my Church, to
see in each person my divine nature, to discern my
design. I have not made you all of one kind. I am a
God of variety and each one is a gift to the whole.

The beauty of holiness

Taste and see that I am good. My beauty is the beauty of the morning, a new beginning, fresh and full of promise. It is the beauty of a hillside, never walked upon before, affording views that fill the heart with freedom and lead the spirit onward, onward.

There is nothing between you and heaven but your humanity, which I will transform into the image of my deity, until it becomes the humanity which I had before the beginning of the world: God on a cross from alpha to omega, the Lamb caught in the thicket of time, the favour of the Almighty for ever poured out for the sake of everything he has made. This is my love for you, all you who need me, all who live in the valley at the foot of the hill.

My beauty is not my own, it is the beauty of your nature that I have freely taken, the beauty that I gave to you when you existed only in my heart.

Pristine beauty is mine and beauty despoiled. These are my two kinds of beauty – beauty outside and inside time. Whatever I had on earth is mine in eternity. Mine is the beauty of holiness and the beauty of hands and feet marked by nails – the beauty of love.

Water into wine

Rejoice in every tribulation as if you are in chains for me, a prisoner of the Gospel. There is no misunderstanding, no persecution, no apathy or denunciation that can make you relent. I am with you and my care is around you. The cost of serving me is your wages for the day, so where there is a flowing out of power, let me fill you with my Spirit.

A diet of sweetmeats was never to your taste, but the bread and water of prison lack the body of bread and wine. Can water be a substitute for wine? Do what I say: bring the water to me and let me change it into wine, the wine of rejoicing in the prison of the soul.

Where there is rejoicing there is freedom, because joy is a revelation of my name. Where I am there is joy, and I am most especially with those who suffer for my sake.

Rejoice that you are called by my name. I have come and I will come that your joy may be full.

The breaking down preceding a rich yield

You are like a compost heap. All the vegetable waste
– peelings and outer leaves – are put on to it. There
they lie scattered, each of its own kind, lying where it
fell, untidy and unpromising, awaiting a slow change
from one kind of matter to another kind of matter.

What power can work on the heap to effect the
change? It is the power of unseen organisms, worms
and bacteria, encouraging breakdown and rot,
distributing particles, moisture playing its part and
heat generated.

In time there is a rich black yield, a composite mixture
of soil and peel and leaf, changed into one kind, to
make the earth fertile and productive.

This is my will for you.

A free gift of grace

My cross in an effective remedy for your sin. It makes
you accepted in the Beloved, and since I am Lord of
all, the efficacy of my death and resurrection is not
limited to those who come after. It is like an explosion
which works outwards in all directions throughout time
and space.

I died once for all, a free gift of grace to the sons and
daughters of the earth. How tenderly passionate is my
love.

Everyone, when he stands with arms outstretched,
makes himself into the shape of the cross. No other
creature can do this, but only you whom I have made
in my own image. Since I have given you dominion
over the whole creation you must include the whole
creation in your response to me.

Place a cross at the top of every mountain and at the
source of every spring. Place crosses to the East for the
sunrise and to the West for the setting of the sun.
Place a cross where every sparrow falls to its death,
and one for every melted flake of snow. These are
treasured in my heart for ever; in this way I will keep
all that I have made.

The laughter and songs of earth

O let the whole earth praise the Lord for his goodness.
Mountains and hills I have raised up to speak of my
grandeur; valleys and plains tell of the protection that I
give. Flowers and fruit and grains shout of the richness
of my blessing, and all creatures that are alive do my
bidding.

You whom I have made in my own image, listen to
the laughter and songs of the earth. Listen also to the
weeping and the dirges. . . and know that I am God.

I give and I take away. I build up and I pull down.
Bless me for ever, for at the heart of my purpose is
love.

Sun, moon and stars sing and rejoice, day and night,
for my light is an everlasting light and in me there is
no darkness at all.

When you praise me you praise the Source of all
goodness, the One who has the whole earth in his
hands. He who blessed the little children and would
not betray their trust will bring all the earth and its
peoples and all the richness that you love, the gaiety of
evening and the stillness of the dawn, the pangs of
birth and death – all to a great rejoicing, not to be
taken away but to be transformed in that heaven of
heavens for which I will transform you, body and soul.

Since my purpose is very good, when you see it, even
now, rejoice.

Become free together

A band tied tightly round your wrist will stop the
supply of blood, and your hand will become numb. A
sapling tied tightly to a support will cut off its own
supply of sap as it grows. Its leaves will be sparse and
pale and it will not flourish. A delphinium tied tightly
to a stake, so that all its stalks are bent, looks
unnatural and will die before it flowers.

I do not want you to be tied too tightly together. Hold
each other in bonds of love as I hold you. Depend on
me and on each other but don't be anyone's jailer.
Become free together – free with the life that I have
given, that never constricts but always lets you grow.

Serve me and serve each other for love of me. To one
I will call with a voice of thunder; to another I will call
like the tinkle of the running brook.

To one I will give the clamour of the market place; to
another a work that is hidden and quiet.

To one I will give pre-eminence of intellect, and to
another the wisdom of the heart.

All of you grow as you receive my Spirit, and as you
lay at my feet the gifts I have given.

The bonds in which I hold you are like the love of a
mother who lets her growing child learn to use his
freedom, like the love of a father who rejoices at the
free affirmation of faith made by his son.

The wounds of love

I can do all things and I strengthen you, and this
strength is not hard and unyielding but soft and warm,
bringing peace and joy.

You receive this strength when you yield yourself to
me. I will liquefy your heart with the depth of your
suffering but I will make your will like steel to endure.

I will melt your bones with the world's pain but I will
make you stand like ancient stone.

When you submit to my will, which you cannot in any
way resist, your acceptance, glad and free, enables you
to receive suffering as blessing, pain as love.

I bear the wounds of love in my body eternally, and
these are the wounds I ask you to bear for love of me.

If you love me you will let me wound you with the
holy wounds with which you wounded me.

All that is is in me

I am eternally begotten of the Father, one with him in the glory of the eternal God.

I am eternally in my creation. I am the Word through whom all things were made.

Everything that I have made I inhabit. All that is has life through my Spirit. All that is is in me.

I am eternally incarnate in my creation through the Word made flesh, conceived by the power of the Holy Spirit in the womb created by my own hand. I am God with you. I am your God who lives in you.

My hand has caused stars to shine in the furthest parts of the universe. I have placed the pebbles at the side of the unknown track. I ensure that you do not forget to breathe, and I remember all the life that has formed the dust of the earth.

It is my love that has kissed the earth into life. In my act of creation was my incarnation and the redemption of the world by my love.

As you cannot escape the reality of the world so you cannot escape my reality. I am more real than the world I have made because its being depends on me.

Forgiveness

Forgiveness is like an arm that you stretch out in friendship, a hand that strokes the brow of someone sick with a fever.

It is like the first gasp of air breathed in by a drowning man as his head breaks above the surface of the water.

It is like an unexpected hour of peace in a day full of cares. It is a blessing given by a dying man. It is life to the one who gives and life to the one who receives.

Forgiveness raises up the fallen and heals the sick. It issues from love as water that rushes out when a sluice-gate is opened. When you know your own need for forgiveness and my tender, merciful love you will never withhold forgiveness from another.

You need forgiveness as you need blood flowing in your veins. My blood of the everlasting covenant was shed for you for the forgiveness of your sins. When you drink my blood my forgiveness makes you grow in love for all for whom I shed my blood.

Blood is life and forgiveness is life. When you forgive you give my life to another. The one who gives is like the Son of Man and the one who receives is like a son of God.

Death and resurrection

For all the redeemed – all, all whom I love – for all who are alive in me, all who have the seed of my life in them, I die, I die, again and again.

I am the dying God, dying always out of my love, dying a thousand deaths in each one of you, dying in every petal that falls from a flower.

I die in every ant that is trodden under foot, in every wounded heart when the sword of unkindness plunges in.

I have chosen to die for you so that your wounds may be healed. When you are hurt I am the One who feels your pain. I die, the just for the unjust, the strong for the weak, made weak so that you may become strong.

What is this gift of mine but the life of the living God? By my dying you live; by my living you learn how to die.

Dying and living pull you apart and make you whole. When you make the sign of the cross you draw upon your body my death and I bring life to your body and soul.

My cross is the instrument of unity

When you are held close to someone you love you can feel the brush of eyelashes against your cheek. When you are close to me there is no knowledge of me but through the heart, the heart that listens and the heart that looks, the heart that desires me and finds its joy in me.

I am the emptiness and the fullness of your heart because I inspire seeking and finding, asking and receiving. I am eternal fullness, perfect and complete, but you need to know your emptiness in order to be filled.

When you need me I am there. When you call me I will come. When you are silent in the wonder of love I am all love in you.

When I ask, you give. When I call, you come. There is never any doubt that you are mine and I am yours because love comes out of trust and trust gives rise to love.

It is my gift to you to know me, now and always. I have made you for myself because I, myself, am for you.

As I unite in my nature God and man so I unite all that is earthly with all that is heavenly, all that is created with the Creator. My cross is the instrument of unity, the horizontal and the vertical that make together one sign that all things are one in me.

The music of love

Lord I will sing to you the songs of true love, because it is your love, not mine, that I sing of.

I will sing to you with the voices of a thousand kings praising you for your magnificence.

I will sing to you with the voices of children praising you because you are kind.

I will sing with the whole of my life – a progression of chords, thick and substantial, like the roots of the mountains, like the ramifications of the hills.

I will sing with a melody like the line of the horizon, like the flight of birds that soar against the clouds.

Blue flecked with the gold of sunlight is the colour of the music – blue for obedience and gold for glory. It is the music of your cross, and I join my voice with all your creation to praise you for the wonder of your love, shown in such a small cross that yet reaches to the ends of the universe.

The wood of the cross is brown like the earth it came from. Brown is my colour, but now my song is blue and gold because you have given me a new song, you have put a song of praise upon my lips.

For ever and ever I will praise you. On earth and in heaven this will be my joy.

Present yourselves to me

I will strengthen your hands held up in prayer to the
One whose hands are held out in blessing over all he
has made. In sweet sounds and sighs and silence
present yourselves to me in adoration and in praise.

Nothing that you ask will be too much when your
supplication is for my sake and according to my will.
Wilful damage, in my divine pity, will become the
grace of sins forgiven, and all that has suffered
negligence will be restored by my tender care.

Leaves that are burnt smoulder and turn to ashes.
Leaves that are composted turn to dust. Fire and rot
bring about, in a flash or by a slow process, a return
to the earth of what grew out of the earth.

In the same way you are of me, you are nourished by
me and you return to me.

The stallion of the night

Wishing and longing are two different things. I inhabit the longings of your heart. They are planted there by my Spirit. They are deep and real.

What you long for will be fulfilled in me – is already fulfilled in the heart that is set on me. What you wish for is of yourself; it is on the surface. Wishing is sterile, like a landscape without vegetation, like an antibiotic that kills the beneficial as well as the harmful bacteria.

If wishes were horses beggars would ride, but the longing heart that finds its fulfilment in me rides on the glory of the morning and is carried on the brightness of the day.

There is no reining in of this steed, but the whole of creation is his heath, galloping above the clouds amongst the galaxies and taking his rest in the stables of the stars.

I am the stallion of the night that will carry you off to an unknown destination. Accustom yourself to my bounding motion and ask not where but why. This journey will answer the question that rings through the universe. You will find the answer when you trust yourself to me.

Life through death

Precious in my sight is the death of your own self. By this death I bring to life your true self that exists in me. You must diminish so that I may increase in you.

By great pain, by agony, the quick of yourself is exposed and tortured into submission. When you shrink from the pain you cannot grow. If you seek to protect your own self from the assaults of my Spirit which come to you through those who touch you in my name, your true self will wither away.

You must be fearless in the face of this onslaught. You must stand and receive the blows which in my wisdom I deal to you.

By coming into the open, by remaining in the line of fire, by allowing me to cut the nerves and tie up the supply of blood with a tourniquet, your own self will yield to your true self – the One who is your strength and your salvation, Christ in you, the hope of glory, your God for ever working within you the resurrection of the dead.

May I come home with you?

Look! I have come to save you. Perfect in my humility
I have come. I am here. I am not only great in glory
above the heavens, but I am small, also, on the earth.

Through the obedient heart of my mother whose will
was submitted to me, I submitted myself to all
humanity. I am the child in your midst, dependent on
you for shelter. I have nowhere to lay my head, no
house to call my own.

May I come home with you? O take me to your heart.
If you refuse I shall die of cold and unkindness.

Have pity on me and give me what I need, if not out
of pity then out of love, love for the God who is
hidden in the guise of guilt – your guilt projected on
to all who suffer at your hands.

If you are innocent then I am guilty. If I am guilty
then you are innocent. This is the divine interchange
that I have decreed so that you should be saved from
your sin.

Look! I am with you but too small to see. Let me
grow in your heart and you will find me there.

All will call me their own

There is no condemnation left upon the face of the earth. It is all wiped away like flour that is spilt on the table, like a swathe that is cut in a field of corn and then the whole field is harvested.

I stand between you and the Holy One, I, Jesus the Righteous One. I have given you my righteousness, I have saved you from your sin. I am your Judge to restore you and to raise you up. The whole earth and all its peoples are in me – they are my tribute. They will follow me wherever I go because I am good, and where I am, there they will be.

As the eyes of a little child look to his mother, and in her presence he finds all he needs, so the eyes of all peoples will look to me and find in me their fulfilment. Because I am crucified and risen all, all, will love me and call me their own.

All whom I acknowledge before the Father as ransomed and healed will worship and adore the One who has taken away their smart. For the sake of your good I have saved you, for the sake of my love.

My light illuminates every dark crevice

Further from your heart than the furthest parts of the universe I dwell in unimaginable light. My goodness is beyond your conceiving, my sweetness you cannot know, until you turn and see me hanging upon the cross, dying for your blindness to make you good.

When I open your eyes it is a spiritual awakening. The Light of the world shines into your heart and illuminates every dark crevice. The whole earth is full of my glory.

The earth is yours and I am yours; time is yours and eternity is yours. I am yours because I am for you. I have given you back yourself remade and my goodness is my gift to you – not your goodness but mine.

The whole creation is alive with my life, and everything that I have made sings praises to its Creator. Woodland and hillside, seashore and the dust of many a pathway bear the footmarks of the Saviour.

Without rancour he has passed this way. There, where you stand this day, is his home country. He is nowhere a stranger but everywhere a guest. He came to his own and he has given it all to you. It is the smallest part of my giving of myself on the cross.

Where is the place where I am not? Search in your heart and see if there is any such place.

We will go together, you and I

Going forward and looking backward will cause you to trip over a fallen branch or to wrench your ankle in a rut. Leave what is behind you and turn and look ahead.

As day succeeds to day you will see the path unfold. Where the way is lost behind the long grass and the banks of hedge parsley, where the undulations of the land hide all but a small scar grazed on the upward slope and visible as a sandy track amongst the rolling green, trust that thousands have trodden this way before and reached the promised land.

Do not wish to find the metalled road that is wide and well marked. This way, though you seem to walk alone, is quiet and I am with you.

Listen to me in your heart and hear me say, "This is the way; walk in it". The way for you starts from here, from this place where your feet are upon the earth.

You do not have to search for the place where the crowds jostle, and mechanised transport thunders along the route. This is the way for you. Look ahead. We will go together, you and I. I am your companion and your destination. I am the Way and the End.

The key

The key is the cross. It is the key to life and death and life. As a key unlocks and locks and unlocks, so my cross gives and takes away and gives again. This key is the key to death and hell, the key to eternal life.

This key does not turn, but the world turns and your hearts turn. My cross is still; it is immovable. It moved me to obedience and it will move you.

The key which is the cross fits every hole or gap or chasm, every void and every empty place. There is a space in your heart which my cross exactly fits, and nothing else can open your life to me.

This key has been forged by an act of my will. It cannot be lost. As an easy turn of the right key raises the tumbler and lets the bolt slip back cleanly, so my cross is effective, and cleanly turns back all that is contrary to my purpose.

Hold this key in the palm of your hand, hang it on a string round your neck, pin it on to your inner clothing, place it in a secure pocket of your purse. Keep it on a ledge above your door and under a stone beside your path.

I have given you the key with which I created goodness out of nothing, by which I turned back the darkness. Keep this key in your heart. It is the key by which I have given you eternal life.

Joy that will never fade

Joy I have given you, joy that will never fade, joy that I am who I am, joy that I have done what I have done, joy because I am for you and not against you, joy because I have taken upon myself the responsibility for your sin.

This is joy: to receive my new life, to be satisfied with length of days in my presence.

This is joy, to celebrate the feast from which no one is excluded, to praise the name by which everyone is saved, to exchange tokens of love with the One who loved the world into being, to kneel before the One who was pierced for all.

This is joy: salvation for every creature, won on the cross by God made man.

This is joy: to give thanks for so great a Saviour, to know him by the outpouring of his grace and love.

The oil of gladness

I will bathe you with the oil of compassion and
healing, not just your feet but all of you. It will be like
the oil that anointed David, and ran down over his
brown hair on to his shoulders, making him a King for
ever.

When you bear upon your forehead the sign of the
cross marked in oil, glistening, warm and smooth, the
oil that has been blessed for healing blesses you. The
oil of my Spirit is the oil of gladness. It is the cross
that marks you, for in the cross is your joy.

Stand under this oil as in a shower. Let it drench you
from head to foot. Let it seep into your clothing and
spread as a pool around your feet. Let the balm of this
unguent sink into your pores and let it soothe your
hurt. What is tight will become supple, what is brittle,
soft.

There is no stinting with this oil. It will drip from
your eyebrows over your eyes and run into your ears.

I will anoint you with my truth and you will see and
hear that I am the King of glory, the anointed One
who anoints all who worship me.

The oil that I pour upon you is precious and good for
healing. It is the oil of salvation.

Bring heaven down to earth

Find in your heart the amalgamation of heaven and earth. Heaven is all around you and the earth is beneath your feet.

Constant prayer, constant sacrifice and a life of constant love – these bring heaven down to earth like the blue sky reflected in a still lake.

Every pool reflects the same sky and even a puddle brings a patch of blue to the ground.

Take me into your calculations and I will show you how to live. Be constant in prayer. Let my Spirit pray in you the prayers of my own heart. Be always ready to be the answer to your prayer.

Be constant in sacrifice and put the needs of others before your own.

Be constant in love. Hate no one for no one is an enemy of the God of love.

This is heaven on earth – prayer and sacrifice and love, a lake of still water where the storms of self-will cannot ruffle the surface, and the blue of obedience shines upwards from earth to heaven.

Cover yourself with psalms

Cover yourself with psalms. There are psalms for all sorts and conditions – psalms of joy and sorrow, psalms of indignation and retort. A psalm is the song of your inmost heart, a song to the God of your life.

Holiness adorns the house where psalms are said and sung, and my holiness adorns you when from your mouth issues forth the praise of my name, and from your heart come question and answer, affirmation and response, threats and imprecations, promise and request.

The psalms that you sing are ever made new in your heart. They speak to your condition of the God who made the earth, who makes you good by his own goodness and gives you a new song to sing.

These songs belong to my people and their sound goes out over all the earth, reaching the ears of countless millions who think they heard the wind pass by.

Sing to your King. You give glory to me when by honest incantation your song is what you are. What you are is the work of my Spirit who gathers songs from the lips of children and places them in my crown.

Rapture is the love that I give

Rapture, pure and simple, is the love that I give. I have come to take you out of yourself into me, so that you may be held by me.

As the needle of a compass always swings to the north, so your heart is attracted by my magnetism.

This rapture is pure – pure joy. It is given by me and directed towards me. It is pure as my Spirit is pure. It is the joy of knowing my love, the only true joy.

It is simple, simple goodness. All goodness is of me and I have made everything good that is good. This is my simplicity: I am he who is good. I gave up myself to come near to you, and in coming near to you I came near to the throne of heaven.

Rapture is the birth of a child, separated from its mother into the world, taking its first breath.

Rapture is a wedding, with the voices of bride and bridegroom speaking promises to one another.

Rapture is death, the final offering of love, summing up all that has gone before, a laying down, pure and simple, a giving over once for all.

After death there is no distraction. The body is wrapped in the grave-clothes as the heart is rapt in me. O joyous day, when you will be pure and simple, like the candle that burns on the altar, white wax with a pure flame burning on top.

A secret garden

You share my life. This gift of my life brings to birth and renews every living thing. I am life and light, life and delight.

When what you are is given by me and given back to me, when you live your life in submission to me, life which seemed to hold no joy is infused with my joy.

It is like a stone wall with a door that has been closed for many years. Suddenly the key is found and the door swings open, giving on to a garden full of pleasant paths and tall trees.

In that garden the flowers bloom whether you see them or not. Behind the stone wall they bloomed unknown to you. Now you see them; then you did not. Now you are joyful; then you were not.

This is the joy of the life I give. It is like a secret garden given by me within your heart.

I am the gardener. In a garden I gave up my life, and in the garden of your heart my risen life calls you by name. I called you into life and I call you into new life.

The paradox of time

Time is a stream that carries you towards me. You are at once in the stream and sitting on the bank observing it.

Time is a film moving across a screen. You are at once in the film and watching it.

Time is a net that I pass through my hands, and the fish that are caught in it are counted by me. It is one face out of a hundred that smiles at you in a crowd so that where many pass by you are conscious of one.

Time goes back and forth, yesterday and tomorrow, and always I am. I, who came into time, am the meaning of time. I am time that stands still.

I bring together the ebb and the flow, the observer and the observed, he who comes and he who goes, the living and the dead, because I was dead and I am alive for evermore.

The world and all that is made is an image of eternity as suffering is an image of glory. One reality exists in another reality – in it and not apart from it.

Time and eternity are one in my cross. I am crucified and I am glorified. I am incarnate and I am ascended. My time is now, and now is the time of your salvation.

Fitting your will to mine

Fitting your will to mine is a misfit, like a row of bent cogs that will not interlock, like a stack of creased paper that will not interleave.

The warp that is in you must be countered by the strength of my love that compels you to look and to lay down your life, and awakens in you a new desire to live for me.

My Spirit, who is the Lord and giver of life, creates and feeds this new life in you.

This life is dependent on love, my love for you and your love given by me, so love and life are one manifestation of my nature. I am he who loves to give life, who gives life to love.

Do not seek your own life but seek me. There is no let or hindrance to my life of love in you but your choice of yourself instead of me. Let me order your life so that what I bring to you in love is accepted by you in love.

Do not be afraid of my will; in all things I do well. The love that you know is good and the best is yet to come.

When I open your eyes to see me, face to face, heart to heart, I in you and you in me, then there will be nothing awry, but all will be straight and sound and utterly fitting, whole and clean and everlasting.

Everything is held together in me

Be conscious of me so that I am in sharp focus at the centre of the picture. My eyes are clear and steady and they look at you with knowledge and with love.

There is a balance in this picture between light and darkness, between what is coloured and what is obscure.

In the foreground is one bud on a branch, beginning to open, and in the background is a forest thick with trees. The bud is the delicate pink of magnolia in the morning, and the forest is the grey-green evening haze of pines.

Between the morning and the evening is the figure of the Christ, between the foreground and the background, between the detail and the haze, between the artist and the picture, between the pray-er and the prayer.

I am your Christ, Christ for you, Christ in the eye of the beholder, Christ who looks out of the picture, Christ who draws you in, Christ who holds your gaze, Christ who forgives your sin.

I hold everything together in myself so that in relation to me nothing is out of place, nothing amiss. Because I am, the picture is complete.

The laughter of God

I am he who laughs in the morning with an eternal *jubilate* that pours from my heart upon the whole creation. I laugh with the light of my love for the liturgy of the whole world in this day's work. I laugh with the laughter of a clown because I have turned the whole world upside down.

I am the open secret, the story of your lost childhood now found.

I am the bread of the hungry, the wisdom of fools, the strength of the weak.

This is why I laugh: who on earth would imagine that heaven is here in your hearts?

I came to the earth as one who laughs behind his hand, and when I opened my arms wide I smiled at you and laughed to be your joy.

You are the company of those who laugh with the kindness of your King. Such laughter is sweet pleasure, rest to your body and soul. Laugh, then, and listen to the laughter of the whole earth that distils from the daisy as it opens its rays to the morning, that roars from the breakers as they crash on to the shore, that ripples across the landscape as it basks in the mid-day sun.

It issues from those who endure hardship and suffering as the inverse of their condition, the hidden dimension which will be made known, the reality at the heart of the universe, where laughter is inhalation instead of exhalation, and I am the One who is inhaled.

The waters which wash clean

Look out over the world and see that it is covered with a sea of ink, a blue dye, thick and indelible, that stains everything that I have made.

You think that by bathing yourself in ink, you will appear vested in the blue of obedience, but this dye proves your guilt and makes plain your deceitful heart.

It is a dye that you cannot wash off. Every river and every stream, the greatest ocean and the smallest spring, is infected. When you wash and when you drink you are stained on the outside and on the inside.

There is a fountain that runs red with blood, that rises from a cross set up on a hill and runs down to cover all the earth. This is the sea of blood which will wash away all your iniquity and cleanse you from your sin.

Every race on earth appeared marked with the same blue stain, but now you shine forth in your true colours, the rich variety that I have made, each one clothed in the blue of my obedience, an obedience that is given, not stolen.

You are as you are, and as you are I have given you myself.

The vulnerability of love

I will have you on any terms. You do not have to
renounce one thing before you come to me.

I will receive you as you are – more, I will come to
you. I am all-giving, all-bestowing.

I do not say: "Repent and then I will look at you. Be
perfect first and then I will accept you." No, I am
humble of heart and I am your advocate. I love you as
you are and I gladly accept you.

What good is repentance that is forced? Anything that
is not free is false. If you want me to change your
heart I will change you by knowing me. The desire for
change must be the free gift of your free heart.

I have not come to put you in chains, to bind you to
obedience, but to fill you with my grace, my utterly
loving gift, that sets you free to love where before you
were bound to yourself.

It is no bargain that I strike with you. I lay my life at
your feet. Do with me what you will.